Longer than Forevermore

By Martha Sears West

We can even find stars in this book.

CLEAN KIND WORLD Los Angeles · Distributed by Ingram Book Company
Copyright © 2019 by Martha Sears West.
Longer Than Forevermore. All rights reserved. Library of Congress Control Number 2102953788
ISBN: 978-0-9886784-2-2 (casebound); 978-1-4774012-3-9 (softbound)
CleanKindWorldBooks.com   ParkPlacePress.com   ymaddox@CleanKindWorldBooks.com
Toll Free 800·616·8081 · Shipping 435·764·4545 · Fax 323·953·9850
2016 Cummings · Los Angeles CA 90027
All titles are available online and in fine bookstores. The Hetty series is available in print, audio, and eBook.
Jake, Dad and the Worm · Longer Than Forevermore · Rhymes and Doodles from a Wind-up Toy
Hetty · Hetty Happens · Hetty or Not · Honeymoon Summer · Hetty on Hold

10 9 8 7 6 5 4
Printed in the United States of America

*longer than the silver river
slowly winding by.*

when morning comes, at noon, or in the still and starry night.

Sometimes, when you're in your bed,
we like to take a peek
and tuck the covers 'round you
all comfy, while you sleep.

We wonder: In your dreams, do you imagine you are big, eating nuts and berries in a hideaway you dig?

and reading books while nestled in a polka dotted chair,

smelling popcorn in the air.

The weather changes often, like the hands upon a clock.

When warmth
has changed to cold,
we change to soft and wooly socks.

But
one thing
never changes

and will last forevermore:

We'll love you still
when you are grown,
exactly as before.

And we will love you bigger

than the biggest things you see,

and longer
than the longest thing
you think could ever be.

More than all the grains of sand,
which we could never count.

And if we add them all...

You were a good listener!

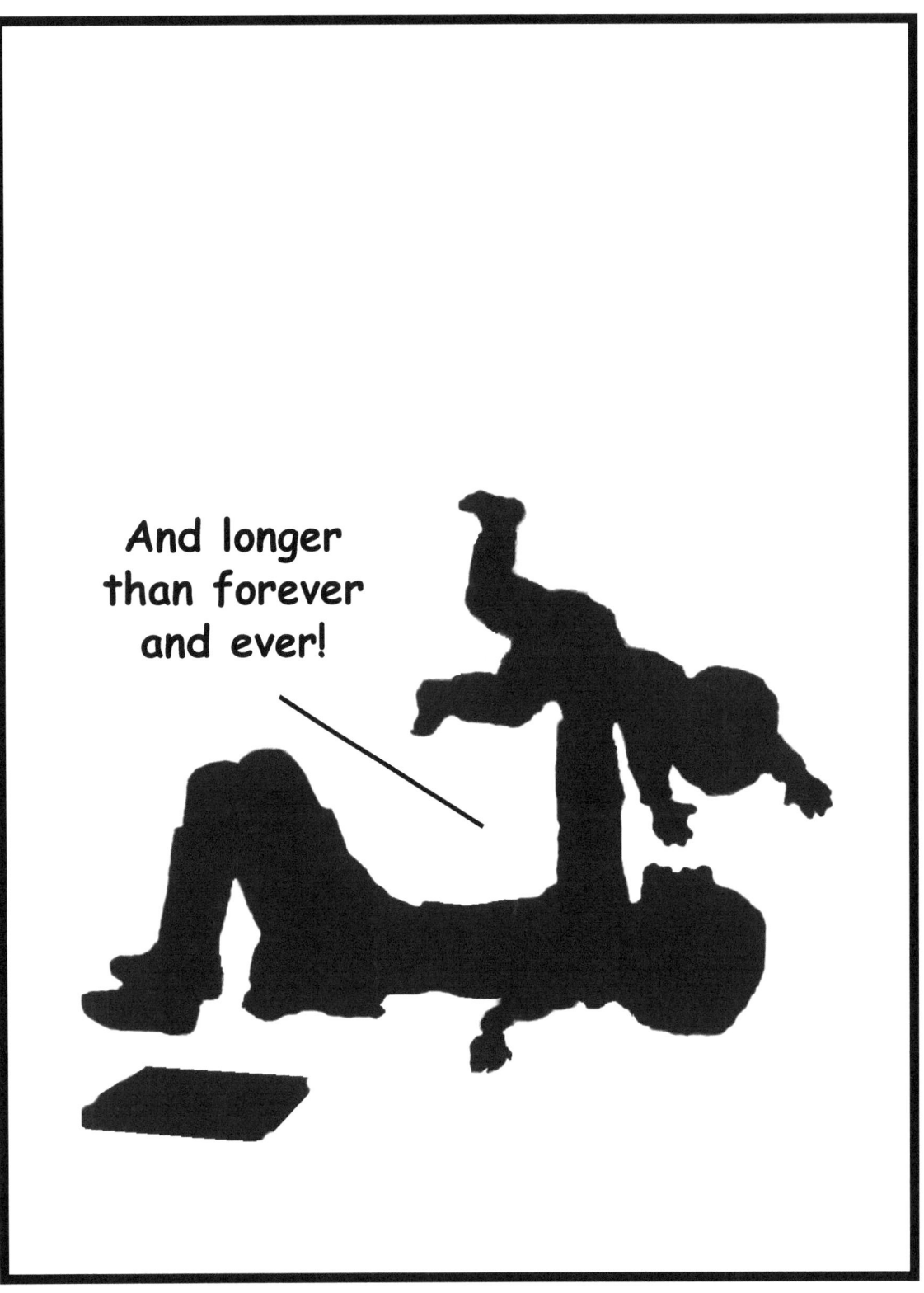

* You might find 57 star shapes, if you look carefully throughout the book.

www.ingramcontent.com/pod-product-compliance
Lightning Source LLC
Chambersburg PA
CBHW041121300426
44112CB00003B/51